Lacy Sunshine's Feathered Tangled Gems Coloring Book

Illustrated by
Heather Valentin

I0410738

This Book
Belongs To

_____

www.ingramcontent.com/pod-product-compliance
Lightning Source LLC
Chambersburg PA
CBHW081752280526
45789CB00008B/2829